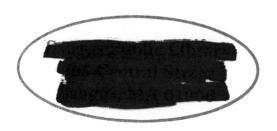

Delightful
DEVON REXES

SILLY! UNIQUE! ACTIVE!

PLAYFUL! DEVOTED! ALERT!

ABDO
Publishing Company

Katherine Hengel

Consulting Editor, Diane Craig, M.A./Reading Specialist

visit us at www.abdopublishing.com

Published by ABDO Publishing Company, a division of ABDO, P.O. Box 398166, Minneapolis, Minnesota 55439. Copyright © 2012 by Abdo Consulting Group, Inc. International copyrights reserved in all countries. No part of this book may be reproduced in any form without written permission from the publisher. Super SandCastle™ is a trademark and logo of ABDO Publishing Company.

Printed in the United States of America, North Mankato, Minnesota
062011
092011

 PRINTED ON RECYCLED PAPER

Editor: Liz Salzmann
Content Developer: Nancy Tuminelly
Cover and Interior Design and Production:
  Anders Hanson, Mighty Media
Illustrations: Bob Doucet
Photo Credits: Shutterstock

Library of Congress Cataloging-in-Publication Data
Hengel, Katherine.
  Delightful Devon rexes / authored by Katherine Hengel ; illustrated by Bob Doucet.
    p. cm. -- (Cat craze. Set 2)
  ISBN 978-1-61714-830-9
  1. Rex cat--Juvenile literature. I. Doucet, Bob, ill. II. Title.
  SF449.R4H465 2012
  636.8'22--dc22
                        2010053267

Super SandCastle™ books are created by a team of professional educators, reading specialists, and content developers around five essential components—phonemic awareness, phonics, vocabulary, text comprehension, and fluency—to assist young readers as they develop reading skills and strategies and increase their general knowledge. All books are written, reviewed, and leveled for guided reading, early reading intervention, and Accelerated Reader® programs for use in shared, guided, and independent reading and writing activities to support a balanced approach to literacy instruction.

CONTENTS

The Devon Rex	3
Facial Features	4
Body Basics	5
Coat & Color	6
Health & Care	8
Attitude & Behavior	10
Litters & Kittens	12
Buying a Devon Rex	14
Living with a Devon Rex	18
Kirlee's Father	20
Find the Devon Rex	22
The Devon Rex Quiz	23
Glossary	24

The
DEVON REX

Devon rexes are far from ordinary.
Their large eyes and ears are unique! So is
their short, curly fur. Devon rexes have a lot
of energy. They like to be silly and have fun.
They act sort of like monkeys!

FACIAL FEATURES

Head

The Devon rex has a triangular head. Its neck is long and thin.

Muzzle

Devon rexes have short **muzzles**. Their **whisker pads** are round and full.

Eyes

A Devon rex has large, oval eyes. The eyes can be any color.

Ears

Their ears are very large and wide. They sit low on the cats' heads.

4

BODY BASICS

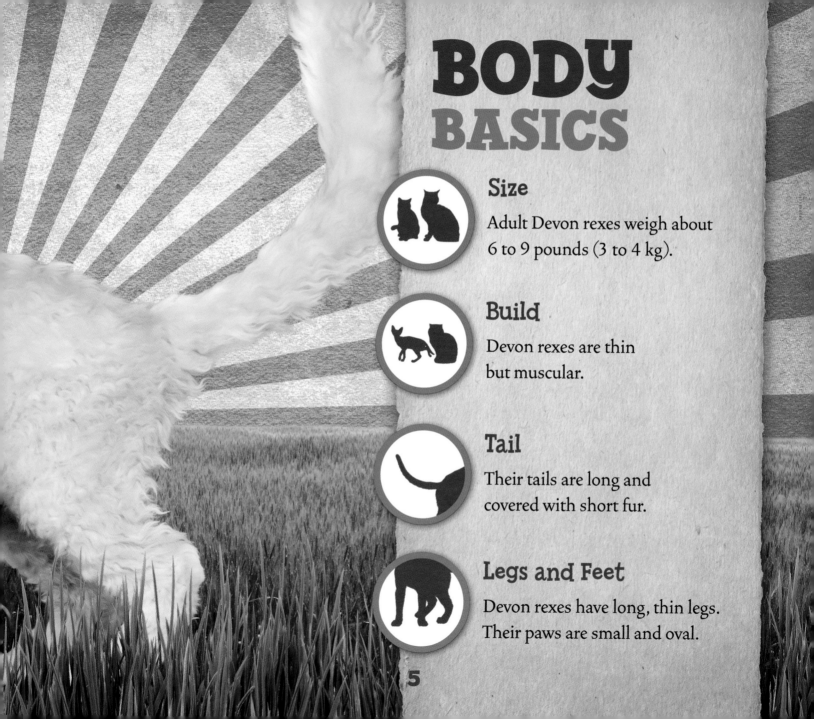

Size
Adult Devon rexes weigh about 6 to 9 pounds (3 to 4 kg).

Build
Devon rexes are thin but muscular.

Tail
Their tails are long and covered with short fur.

Legs and Feet
Devon rexes have long, thin legs. Their paws are small and oval.

COAT & COLOR

Devon Rex Fur

It's fun to pet a Devon rex! Their short coats are wavy and soft. That's because their coats don't have many guard hairs. Guard hairs are coarse. Since Devon rexes don't have many, they feel extra soft!

Devon rexes also feel warm. Their body temperature is the same as other cats. But you can feel their body heat more because of their light coats. Some Devon rexes have a lot of loose curls. Others have thinner coats. The amount of fur they have can change as they grow.

BLACK FUR

BLACK

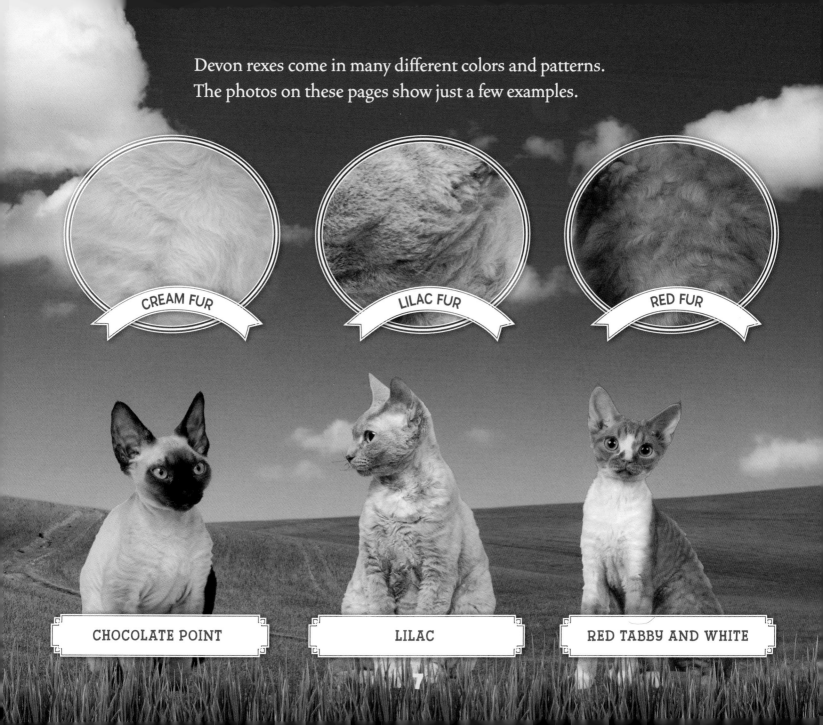

Devon rexes come in many different colors and patterns. The photos on these pages show just a few examples.

CREAM FUR

LILAC FUR

RED FUR

CHOCOLATE POINT

LILAC

RED TABBY AND WHITE

HEALTH & CARE

Life Span

Devon rexes can live
for 10 to 15 years.

Health
Concerns

Devon rexes should be
kept inside. Their light
coats don't protect them
very well. They can easily
get too hot or too cold.

Devon rexes can have
genetic problems. But
most Devon rexes are
very healthy cats.

8

VET'S CHECKLIST

- Have your Devon rex spayed or neutered. This will prevent unwanted kittens.

- Visit a vet for regular checkups.

- Ask your vet which types of food and litter are right for your Devon rex.

- Clean your Devon rex's teeth and ears once a week.

- Ask your vet about shots that may benefit your cat.

ATTITUDE & BEHAVIOR

Personality

Devon rexes are very loving. They enjoy being held, and they love to be petted! They are outgoing and always purring. They are also very curious and alert. Everything interests them!

Activity Level

Devon rexes are very active! They like to play with their owners. They are very good jumpers. They'll even jump in the shower! They can climb just about anything too.

All About Me

Hi! My name is Dominique. I'm a Devon rex. I just wanted to let you know a few things about me. I made some lists below of things I like and dislike. Check them out!

Things I Like

- Getting in the shower with people
- Crawling under the covers
- Being held and petted
- Begging for table scraps
- Sleeping in warm places
- Cuddling with my owner
- Climbing and jumping

Things I Dislike

- Being outside in the cold
- Being alone
- Being ignored
- Missing my owners
- Getting bored
- Being outside in the hot sun

LITTERS & KITTENS

Litter Size

A female Devon rex usually gives birth to three to five kittens.

Diet

Newborn kittens drink their mother's milk. They can begin to eat kitten food when they are about six weeks old. Kitten food is different from cat food. It has the extra **protein**, fat, **vitamins**, and **minerals** that kittens need to grow.

Growth

Devon rex kittens should stay with their mother until they are two to three months old. A Devon rex will be almost full grown when it is six months old. But it will continue to grow slowly until it is about one year old.

BUYING A DEVON REX

Choosing a Breeder

It's best to buy a kitten from a **breeder**, not a pet store. When you visit a cat breeder, ask to see the mother and father of the kittens. Make sure the parents are healthy, friendly, and well behaved.

Picking a Kitten

Choose a kitten that isn't too active or too shy. If you sit down, some of the kittens may come over to you. One of them might be the right one for you!

Is It the Right Cat for You?

Buying a cat is a big decision. You'll want to make sure your new pet suits your lifestyle.

Get out a piece of paper. Draw a line down the middle.

Read the statements listed here. Each time you agree with a statement from the left column, make a mark on the left side of your paper. When you agree with a statement from the right column, make a mark on the right side of your paper.

Left	Right
I like active cats. ☐	☐ I don't want my cat to climb and jump on things.
Cuddling with a cat is great! ☐	☐ I don't like to cuddle with cats.
Cats with soft coats are cool! ☐	☐ I like cats that have a lot of fur.
I want a cat that likes to be around me. ☐	☐ I want a cat that occupies itself.
I don't need to take my cat outside. ☐	☐ I would like to take my cat outside in all kinds of weather.

If you made more marks on the left side than on the right side, a Devon rex may be the right cat for you! If you made more marks on the right side of your paper, you might want to consider another **breed**.

Some Things You'll Need

Cats go to the bathroom in a **litter box**. It should be kept in a quiet place. Most cats learn to use their litter box all by themselves. You just have to show them where it is! The dirty **litter** should be scooped out every day. The litter should be changed completely every week.

Your cat's **food and water dishes** should be wide and shallow. This helps your cat keep its whiskers clean. The dishes should be in a different area than the litter box. Cats do not like to eat and go to the bathroom in the same area.

Cats love to scratch! **Scratching posts** help keep cats from scratching the furniture. The scratching post should be taller than your cat. It should have a wide, heavy base so it won't tip over.

Cats are natural predators. Without small animals to hunt, cats may become bored and unhappy. **Cat toys** can satisfy your cat's need to chase and capture. They will help keep your cat entertained and happy.

Cats should not play with balls of yarn or string. If they accidentally eat the yarn, they could get sick.

Cat claws should be trimmed regularly with special cat claw **clippers**. Regular nail clippers will also work. Some people choose to have their cat's claws removed by a vet. But most vets and animal rights groups think declawing is cruel.

A **cat bed** will give your cat a safe, comfortable place to sleep.

LIVING WITH A DEVON REX

Being a Good Companion

Devon rexes don't need a lot of **grooming**. They should be bathed occasionally. You can dry them quickly with just a towel. That's it! Check their large ears once a week. Sometimes they need to be gently wiped clean.

Inside or Outside?

It's a good idea to keep your Devon rex inside. Devon rexes do not have thick fur to keep them warm and protect their skin. Most vets and **breeders** agree that it is best for cats to be kept inside. That way the cats are safe from predators and cars.

Feeding Your Devon Rex

Devon rexes may be fed regular cat food. Your vet can help you choose the best food for your cat.

Cleaning the Litter Box

Like all cats, Devon rexes like to be clean. They don't like smelly or dirty litter boxes. If the litter box is dirty, they may go to the bathroom somewhere else. Ask your vet for advice if your cat isn't using its box.

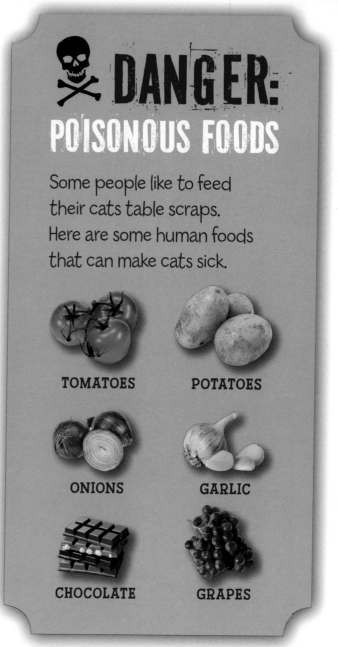

☠ DANGER:
POISONOUS FOODS

Some people like to feed their cats table scraps. Here are some human foods that can make cats sick.

TOMATOES

POTATOES

ONIONS

GARLIC

CHOCOLATE

GRAPES

KIRLEE'S FATHER

In 1959, a straight-coat **calico** had a litter of kittens. They were born in Devon, England. A woman named Beryl Cox found them near her house. All of the kittens had straight coats, except for one male. He had beautiful black and brown curls! Miss Cox named him Kirlee. He would grow up to be the first Devon rex.

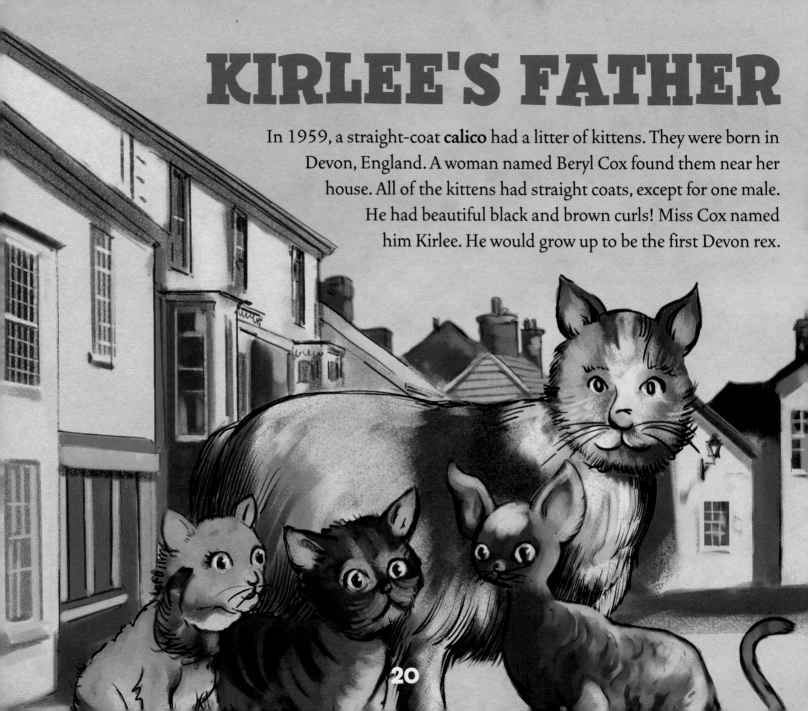

Breeders all around the world were amazed! Where did his curls come from? Kirlee's mother had a straight coat. But who was his father? Miss Cox and others believed they knew.

Around that time, there was a large black cat living near an old tin mine. He was very wild. No one could catch him! But he had beautiful black curls that hung in **ringlets** around his tail. He was probably Kirlee's father.

FIND THE DEVON REX

A

B

C

D

Answers: A) Oriental shorthair B) Devon rex (correct) C) Russian blue D) Scottish Fold

THE DEVON REX QUIZ

1. Devon rexes have a lot of energy. **True or false?**

2. A Devon rex has small eyes. **True or false?**

3. Devon rexes always feel cold when you touch them. **True or false?**

4. Devon rexes don't like to be held or petted. **True or false?**

5. A Devon rex might jump in the shower with you! **True or false?**

6. A cat named Kirlee was the first Devon rex. **True or false?**

GLOSSARY

breed - a group of animals or plants with common ancestors. A *breeder* is someone whose job is to breed certain animals or plants.

calico - a tri-color cat with patches of white, black, and orange.

genetic - having characteristics passed from one generation to another.

groom - to clean the fur of an animal.

mineral - a natural element that plants, animals, and people need to be healthy.

muzzle - the nose and jaws of an animal.

protein - a substance found in all plant and animal cells.

ringlet - a long curl of hair.

vitamin - a substance needed for good health, found naturally in plants and meats.

whisker pad - an area on the side of an animal's muzzle that whiskers grow out of.